D1251105

TOTALLY GROSS HISTORY™

THE TOTALLY GROSS HISTORY OF
ANCIENT EGYPT

TRACEY BAPTISTE

rosen publishing's
rosen central

Published in 2016 by The Rosen Publishing Group, Inc.
29 East 21st Street, New York, NY 10010

First Edition

Library of Congress Cataloging-in-Publication Data

Baptiste, Tracey, author.
 The totally gross history of ancient Egypt / Tracey Baptiste. — First edition.
    pages cm. — ((Totally gross history))
 Includes bibliographical references and index.
 ISBN 978-1-4994-3754-6 (library bound) — ISBN 978-1-4994-3752-2 (pbk.) —
 ISBN 978-1-4994-3753-9 (6-pack)
 1. Egypt—Civilization—To 332 B.C. 2. Egyptians—Health and hygiene—History. I. Title.
 DT61.B3225 2015
 932.01—dc23
                                            2015025919

Manufactured in the United States of America

CONTENTS

INTRODUCTION

What we think of as Ancient Egypt is a period of 3,000 years, representing one of the longest-lasting civilizations. The pyramids that were built at the beginning of the rule of the pharaohs were ancient even to Egyptians living at the end of the time of pharaohs! Ancient Egyptians were responsible for some truly incredible things. They were one of the first civilizations to have a navy. They were the first people in the world to have an irrigation system. They dug canals to direct water from the Nile to farms. They built reservoirs to hold water during the dry season. They were among the first people to grow crops and breed livestock. A calendar helped the farmers predict the annual flooding of the Nile. Because the height of the floodwater determined the fate of farmers for the rest of the year, they developed a system of measurement using stone gauges called nilometers. They also developed mathematical formulas to record the heights of floods.

Ancient Egyptians recorded information about floods, formulas, and finances with one of the first systems of written communication, called hieroglyphics. They were some of the world's first astronomers, and used this knowledge to build the great pyramids, positioning them according to the heavens.

Mummification gave them practical information about how the body worked, and they had well-developed medicines and even surgery. There were also dentists. But the

Mummies are the dessicated remains of Ancient Egyptians. The earliest mummies dried naturally and were often found with arms and legs pulled up against the body.

Ancient Egyptians had a strict social class system with the wealthy and well-born at the top, and everyday people and slaves at the bottom.

The Ancient Egyptians were incredible. They were smart, inventive, and knowledgeable, but they also did a lot of strange things. They kept slaves, their laws allowed them to maim offenders, and a brother and sister could marry each other. This resource is filled with facts that show how amazing, and gross, the Ancient Egyptians really were.

CHAPTER ONE

YOU DON'T HAVE TO BE FAIR TO BE PHARAOH

The rule of the pharaohs began around 3100 BCE when King Menes of Upper Egypt conquered Lower Egypt. King Menes made his capital in Memphis, which was located in the former Lower Egypt. From there, he founded cities, oversaw the construction of irrigation systems, introduced the papyrus and writing, and saw the first laws made. Despite all we know about Menes' accomplishments, there is no accurate account of the end of Menes' life. Some historians think that he died of anaphylactic shock, or a severe allergic reaction, from getting stung by a wasp. Others say that he was chased by dogs, fell into a lake, and had an encounter with some crocodiles. All pretty gross ways to go!

THE ROYAL FAMILY HAD IT ROUGH

After Menes, there were only sole rulers of Egypt. To eliminate the competition, pharaohs typically married all the daughters of potential enemies. And no, the women didn't have a choice in the matter. The oldest sons of a pharaoh were destined for the throne. They had strength and combat training, because pharaohs rode at the front of the armies during war. They learned bow and arrow skills, how to ride horses, and tested their endurance in lengthy footraces. They also engaged in dangerous hunts, pitting themselves against wild animals including lions, bulls, antelopes, elephants, and even hippos!

Maintaining physical health was not just good practice, it also helped a pharaoh keep his job! In the Heb-sed festival, a pharaoh had to run a ritual course four times. The festival was held after a pharaoh had ruled for thirty years. But it would be another thirty years to the next festival right? Wrong! Pharaohs who reached this milestone had to run the course every three years from then on.

MILITARY MYSTERIES

At ten years old, Ramses II was made a general, and learned good military strategy. After the death of his father, he engaged in several military campaigns. One of these battles however had a very odd conclusion. At the Battle of Qadesh (c. 1274 BCE), Ramses II and the Hittite Empire clashed in a huge fight. The Hittites split Ramses army, but Ramses counterattacked, which sent the Hittites running. So who actually won this battle? Who knows? Ramses II returned to Egypt claiming victory, and the Hittites returned home saying they had crushed the Egyptians!

Seqenenre Tao, a Seventeenth Dynasty pharaoh, was also no stranger to combat. This poor pharaoh was killed by three head wounds. A blow from an axe cut his cheek, exposed his teeth, and fractured his jaw. Another blow injured his skull. The third, by either a dagger or spear, cut open his forehead above his eye. Historians know he lay dead for a while because the body began to decompose before it was embalmed. But did he die in battle, or asleep in his own bed? Here's what we do know: Somebody did *not* like that pharaoh.

DON'T LET THE POWER GO TO YOUR HEAD

The pharaoh had authority over everyone. He had many servants, and it was such an honor to serve, that when he died, someone bashed his servants on the head so that they could follow the pharaoh into the afterlife to serve him or her. Things weren't much better for live servants either. One king called Pepy II hated to be bugged by flies, so he slathered his slaves in honey so the flies would only bother them. Some honor!

One pharaoh named Akhenaten decided that there was only one god called Aten. There is a story that Akhenaten and one of

This relief, c. 1370–c1330 BCE, shows Nefertiti and Akhenaten with their children. The sun disc Aten is shown above them.

his six daughters by Queen Nefertiti had a fight over this new religion. As a result, he had his own daughter executed. Then, because she believed in the old religion that a person could only go into the afterlife with their entire body, he had one of her hands removed! No one has been able to say whether this story is true. Let's hope it isn't!

Akhenaten spent so much time concerned with Aten that he forgot about defending Egypt. The high priests weren't too happy about that, and Akhenaten came to a sudden and mysterious death. In his place, his younger brother, Tutankhamun became pharaoh. The boy was too young to rule, so his Uncle Ay (also Akhenaten's uncle) became his advisor, which meant Ay was actually ruling Egypt. Some believe that Ay wanted all the power. They use this to explain young Tut's death. Now, all Ay had to do was marry Ankhesenamun, Tut's wife. Only, she was his granddaughter! Talk about gross! Ankhesenamun tried to marry a foreign prince instead. But the prince was murdered on his way to Egypt. She married her grandfather but fortunately, Ay only lived for four more years.

Intermarriage was not uncommon among Egypt's royals. Egyptians did everything they could to keep the power within the family. Of course things did not always work out so smoothly.

When Thutmose II died, his son, Thutmose III, should have become pharaoh, but he was an infant. So Thutmose II's wife, Hatshepsut ruled instead. She wore a fake beard and a king's kilt and ruled for twenty years, building and restoring temples and monuments rather than waging war. After her death, she was known as one of Egypt's most successful pharaohs. But the new pharaoh, Thutmose III, destroyed her monuments. Many

A kneeling statue of Hatshepsut from Hatshepsut's temple at Deir el-Bahri.

of her inscriptions were defaced, and a wall was constructed around her obelisks. Seems like pretty gross behavior! However, Thutmose III wasn't holding a grudge. He most likely wanted to make sure that his son would succeed without any challenge from Hatshepsut's other children.

A LOVE TRIANGLE GONE HORRIBLY WRONG

The last pharaoh, Cleopatra, is also one of the most famous rulers in history. She became pharaoh at age eighteen when King Ptolemy XII died. She married her brother, ten-year-old Ptolemy, so they could rule together, but the two never got along. Cleopatra fled to Syria and returned with an army. At the same time, Julius Caesar came to Egypt from Rome, chasing an enemy. Cleopatra saw her opportunity to get a bigger army, by getting Caesar to join her. Caesar defeated Ptolemy XIII for Cleopatra. Not long after, Cleopatra had a son for Caesar, but he never acknowledged that the child was his.

After Caesar's murder, Marc Antony called Cleopatra to Rome to answer questions about Caesar. The two fell in love and eventually had three children. However, the same civil war that led Julius Caesar to Egypt in the first place was still ongoing. Now, Marc Antony was fighting Octavian, Caesar's nephew. Marc Antony tried to have Cleopatra's son with Caesar declared the rightful heir in order to join Egypt and Rome. But Antony and Cleopatra's armies were defeated. Antony was mistakenly told that Cleopatra had died. He committed suicide by stabbing himself. When Cleopatra heard what happened, she ended her life by allowing herself to be bitten by a snake. They were buried together.

Although Cleopatra had been trying to strengthen Egypt, her actions brought an end to the age of pharaohs.

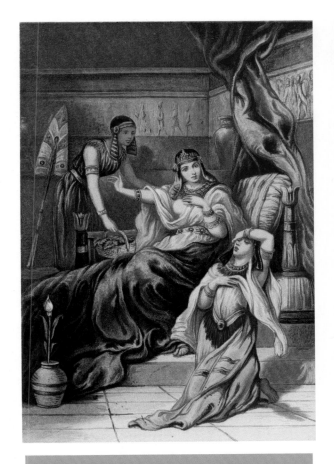

Cleopatra was so famous that William Shakespeare wrote about her in *Antony and Cleopatra*. This illustration of Cleopatra is for an anthology of Shakespeare's works.

CHAPTER TWO

WAX IN YOUR HAIR, FAT ON YOUR SKIN

The life of a pharaoh was hard. Filled with infighting and constant war troubles, it was probably better to be on the lower end of the social structure, right? Maybe not. Here are some pretty nasty examples of what it was like for the rest of the citizens of Ancient Egypt.

THE COMFORTS OF HOME

Egypt is a dry, hot place. In the days before air conditioning, people had to make do with clever building solutions. The very poor lived in reed huts, but most people had houses made of mud with flat roofs and small windows. That kept inside dark, but cool. It also kept the dust and flies out. Roof balconies had vents that directed breeze to anyone sleeping there on hot nights. While the rich owned elaborate furniture, most people had just a chest and some mats or mattresses. It wasn't a very comfortable life. Even their pillows were made of stone.

Ancient Egyptians didn't have bathrooms. They used a seat placed over a jar with sand. When they were finished, they would just throw the contents out in a nearby pit or into the street. Men and women in Ancient Egypt peed differently than we do today. Women stood, while the men squatted.

Most people did not have honey-covered servants to keep flies away. They used flycatchers and flyswatters. Flyswatters were made from horse hair. But the truly fashionable had swatters made from giraffe tails, which were probably not as fashionable for the giraffe!

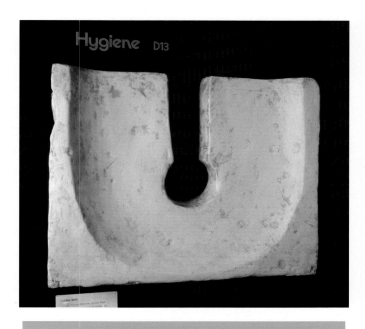

This c. 1370 ceramic toilet seat was found at a shared lavatory in an army camp in El-Amarna, Egypt.

THAT ANIMAL IS LIKE FAMILY

People lived with their animals. Not pets—livestock! Poor people might share their one-room home with these animals. Even the rich had stalls and stables that opened into the same courtyard they used. Imagine the smell!

Archaeologists have found thousands of mummified animals. This tells us that the animals were important to them as more than just food. Paintings show people petting different kinds of animals. But perhaps the most important animal was the cat. Cats were kept as pets but they were also revered. In 1888, 80,000 cat mummies were discovered. Their owners probably expected to be rejoined with them in the afterlife. Some cat mummies were buried with mummified mice and bowls of milk. Killing a cat meant a harsh penalty, even if it happened by accident. People convicted of killing a cat were sentenced to death by poisonous snake pit!

There were zoos in Ancient Egypt. Hatshepsut kept monkeys, leopards, and giraffes. They were buried in the same places as wealthy people. In 2004, the mummy of a lion was found in the tomb of Tutankhamen's wet nurse, Maïa. Ramses II was said to take a lion into battle with him. Akhenaten also kept lions, antelope, and cattle, and had a pond that may have housed fish and water birds.

This mummified cat is in the collection at the Louvre Museum in Paris, France.

FASHION AND HYGIENE

It was so hot in Ancient Egypt that people wore as little as possible. Children often went completely naked. Servants and dancing girls often worked naked. If anyone wore clothing, it was usually made of loose white linen. Hair was also hot and bothersome, so both men and women cut it off with knives. (There were no scissors then.) But the heat of the sun could be tough, so people wore wigs as hats. Sometimes people put large cones of scented wax on top of their wigs. The cones would melt in the heat, releasing perfume and cooling moisture onto the wearer's head.

Both men and women wore makeup. They used kohl, a black makeup that was used to outline their eyes, their eyebrows, and their lashes. Kohl contained the mineral malachite, which helped protect them from eye disease.

Because it was so hot, people sometimes bathed several times a day. Noble women would also have their bodies massaged with oils and perfumes. They used henna, a red dye, to color their nails and hair. Several makeup products have also been uncovered in Ancient Egypt, like pots that contained face cream

This is an example of an Ancient Egyptian headdress and earrings from the 16th to 13th century BCE.

or perfume, mirrors, and makeup applicators. Perfumes were made of combinations of flowers, or scented wood, mixed with oil or animal fat.

FOOD

Living along the Nile River had its perks. Ancient Egyptians had a wide variety of foods available to them such as figs, dates, grapes, lettuce, beans, cucumbers, leeks, and peas. They made bread, and ate meat from cattle, pigs, goat, and sheep. They also had a good supply of fish.

When the rich had banquets, they had all kinds of exotic food. Oxen, duck, geese, and pigeon would be served. At festivals, however, royals and nobles would bring food to share with everyone. For people on the lower end of society, it was their opportunity to taste luxuries like wine and beef.

GOOD FOR THE BELLY, BAD FOR THE TEETH

The most popular food was bread, but making bread was not an easy task. The wheat or barley was harvested, then trampled by cattle to separate the grain from the straw. Then the grain was separated from the chaff by throwing basketfuls of it into the air so the breeze would carry away the chaff. The grain was then ground by women using two large flat stones. The women knelt in front of the stones and rubbed grain between them for hours. Lastly, the flour was baked into flat pancakes. The wealthy might have fancier bread with honey, fruit, or spices, or even with fancy

This illustration shows workers at a royal bakery doing different tasks in the process of baking.

shapes. But as much as the Ancient Egyptians liked their bread, making and eating it was rough on their bodies. The process of grinding on stone meant that bits of sand and stone got into the baked bread. It wore down people's teeth like sandpaper.

PAY ME IN FOOD...OR ELSE!

Beer was very important in Ancient Egypt. Both children and adults drank it. The drink was also mainly made by women, by straining and fermenting bread. Beer was important enough to be used to pay wages. Some workers would get beer as many as three times a day. Another form of payment was beef. Once, in Egypt a group of pyramid workers didn't get their beer and beef on schedule. They complained of being "desperate with hunger and thirst" and threatened to raid a supply warehouse. The plan worked! They were brought their food and drink, and they went back to work. No wonder some of the worker crews had nicknames like "The Drunkards of Menkaure."

THE PORTRAITS ARE DECEIVING

Honey was another favorite food of the Ancient Egyptians. It was expensive to make, so they ate it sparingly—unless they were wealthy. All that beer, bread, and honey wasn't great for the body. While pharaohs and nobles were often portrayed as slender in wall drawings, researchers actually found that most of the people of the time were overweight. Queen Hatshepsut was obese and balding at death.

WEIRD WORKING CONDITIONS

In Ancient Egypt, your social class determined what kind of work you could do. Nobles tended to be architects, mathematicians, astronomers, doctors, and pharmacists. Next, came soldiers,

WERE WORKERS HAPPY?

At least some of the workforce for the pyramids and other architectural projects were slave labor. The Ancient Egyptians also used prisoners of war for labor. Nubians and Asians taken during war were enslaved and sent to work. Some Nubians were used as soldiers to keep others in line.

During a period of civil war when the pharaohs didn't have as much power, laborers went around committing crimes. This suggests that they were quite unhappy with their lives.

then scribes, who kept records, collected taxes, and anything else the royal family requested. Artisans such as painters, sculptors, metalworkers, goldsmiths, and glassmakers came next. Pharaohs kept villages filled with craftspeople whose job was to make things for the tombs. Near the bottom of this class society were laborers who worked on buildings and who also did farm work. That's right, both! Farmers worked on building projects when they couldn't farm. Sometimes farmers would run away and pretend not to hear the vizier calling them for building work. If they were caught, they were beaten.

THE PYRAMID BUILDERS

Laborers who worked on pyramids probably had it the worst of all. The work was backbreaking. Literally. Archaeologists have found skeletons with spinal injuries from carrying huge stone blocks. Many had severe stiffness and swelling from arthritis.

Still, laborers were proud of their efforts. Crews sometimes carved their own praises into the structures they worked on.

WOMEN'S WORK?

Both men and women could handle business deals. Men usually dealt with land and farming, and women usually tended to household duties. Women could also become scribes or doctors if they came from wealthy families and were educated. They could also be employed as entertainers such as dancers, perfume makers, or mourners. Traditionally, women also did the weaving. The loom was horizontal and lay on the floor. Women would kneel to use it. But when a different kind of loom was made so that people could use it standing (which was easier), men started to do the weaving instead. Talk about unfair!

UNUSUAL WORKERS

For some jobs, it paid to be a little bit strange. People with unusual physical traits were almost guaranteed certain kinds of work. Dwarves and "giants" were allowed jobs working with gold. Why? If anything was stolen, people of unusual height would be easier to pick out of a crowd.

WHAT ABOUT FUN?

Archaeologists have found paintings of people doing somersaults and cartwheels, and dancing during festivals. But they also enjoyed swimming, dancing, rode animals, and hunted for sport.

TOYS, GAMES, AND MUSIC

One popular pastime was a game called senet. It was played on a flat board with thirty squares. The game represented a struggle between good and evil. Two players threw numbered sticks in the air, like dice, which helped them decide how to move their pieces. Tjau was another board game that was played on a similar surface to that of senet. One children's game called mehen, which means coiled one, used a board with a spiral pattern. At one end was a snake's tail and the object was to move pieces, either lion shapes or marbles, to the center eye.

Children also played with pull toys and dolls. Babies had rattles, while older children had balls of wood or leather, and toy weapons. Both boys and girls might team up for wrestling matches but boys mostly competed in races and javelin throws, while girls preferred to dance.

Music was also a part of Ancient Egyptian life. Some instruments that have been found include the flute, oboe, and harp. Some harps had elaborate carvings of the pharaohs on them.

HUNTING

Wall paintings show people doing everything from hunting for birds in a papyrus swamp, to hunting gazelles on the back of a chariot. Nobles and royalty enjoyed hunting for fun. There are several images of pharaohs killing hippos in Ancient Egyptian art. Hippos are dangerous. At up to 15 feet (about 4.5 meters) tall, and weighing up to 8,000 pounds (around 3,628 kilograms), they can cause a lot of damage. Though they can't

This ancient painting from a private tomb shows a hippopotamus roaring among papyrus.

be found in Egypt anymore, they once roamed the Nile freely. People went out in boats to hunt them, and the animals could easily capsize boats and injure the people who fell out.

In 2010, Dr. Benson Harer offered up a new theory about King Tut's death. Tutankhamun's body was found with severed ribs and his heart was not embalmed, which was unusual. Dr. Harer believes it is evidence of a crushing injury to the chest. In Tutankhamun's tomb, there are two statues of the young king hunting hippopotamus using a spear. Might this have been King Tut's last act? A run-in with a hippo is a gruesome way to go.

CHAPTER THREE

A THOUSAND GODS AND ABOUT A MILLION MUMMIES

Religion was very important to the Ancient Egyptians. They believed in more than a thousand gods. Well, everyone except Akhenaten, and we all know what happened to him! While all of the gods were considered to be important, some had a higher status than others.

A WHO'S WHO OF ANCIENT GODS AND GODDESSES

Osiris was the king of Egypt. His wife was his sister, Isis. After his brother Set (or Seth) murdered him, Isis used magic to put Osiris back together. They had a son, Horus, whose job it was to avenge his father's murder. Horus eventually became king of Egypt, and Osiris and Isis became king and queen of the underworld.

Isis was the goddess of fertility, healing, the moon, and love. Her act of putting her husband back together with bandages is said to be the foundation of the practice of mummification.

Horus, the god of light and sky, was sometimes shown to have a falcon's head. He avenged his father by killing Set.

Thoth, the god of wisdom, writing, and magic, is the scribe of the underworld who recorded the decision about whether a person was worthy or not. He wrote spells in the *Book of the Dead*, and the *Book of Thoth* held the secrets of the universe.

Ra (or Re), the sun god, is possibly the most important of all. Egyptians believed that the world began anew every day. Ra was brought to life every morning, and died every night.

Set (or Seth), the god of chaos and darkness, had the head of a dog, and a forked tail. He is also sometimes shown as a pig, crocodile, scorpion, or hippopotamus.

Amun (or Amon), the king of the gods, was often shown with a ram's head. Amun was later merged with the god Ra as Amun-Ra. For a time, Amun-Ra was the chief god in Ancient Egypt.

Anubis was the divine embalmer. He also weighed a person's heart to determine if they could go into the afterlife. Anubis is always shown with a jackal's head and black skin.

A statue of Set, c. 1300–1080 BCE, from the Carlsberg Glyptotek Museum in Copenhagen.

Ma'at (or Maat) was the goddess of truth and justice. She was often shown with an ostritch feather on her head, which was called the "feather of truth."

DEADLY SIBLING RIVALRY

Besides Isis and Set, Osiris had another sibling: Nephthys, who became Set's wife. Set was jealous because Osiris and Isis were given rule over Egypt. After Set killed Osiris, and Isis found the body, Set tore Osiris' body into fourteen pieces and scattered it up and down the Nile. Isis and Nephthys found all but one piece. Isis put it together using magic. That was how Osiris became god of the dead.

A HEAVY HEART

After death, Egyptians believed that they were to be judged. This final judgment was called the weighing of the heart. The ceremony determined whether a person had done enough good deeds while they were alive. A person with a heart as light as Ma'at's feather was worthy of the underworld, while

A papyrus shows the ceremony of the weighing of the heart. Anubis checks the scales with the heart on the left and the feather of truth on the right.

one with a heavy heart was not. The heart was weighed by Anubis. If it was heavy, Ammut, with his crocodile head, would eat it. The person would not go to the afterlife. But if the person's heart was light, Horus would present the person to his parents for a happy afterlife in the Field of Reeds.

BEWARE THE JACKAL

Anubis, the embalmer of the gods, probably had a jackal's head because there were lots of jackals in Ancient Egypt. These wild dogs often dug up dead bodies and dismembered them. Jackals came to be closely associated with dead bodies. Anubis also helped Isis put her husband's body back together. Priests wore a jackal mask when they performed mummification ceremonies.

BE GOOD, OR THE CROCODILE WILL EAT YOU

The god Ammut ate the heavy hearts and sent the spirits of bad Ancient Egyptians packing. But he also had another job: scaring the living. If you were behaving badly, Ammut might just show up to eat you on the spot. No waiting to be dead to be judged by him!

WERE THERE ALWAYS MUMMIES?

Early Ancient Egyptians were found buried in sand pits. The heat and dryness of the desert probably dehydrated the bodies quickly. This made the bodies into natural mummies. But because jackals might dig up the bodies for food, people began to

SO MANY MUMMIES, SO MANY USES!

So many mummies were found in the 1800s that people had all kinds of creative uses for them. Which of these do you think mummies were really used for?

a) They were burned as fuel.
b) They were ground up and made into paint.
c) They were used as decorations around the house.
d) They were made into wrapping paper.
e) They were used as fertilizer.

If you guessed any of these, you are correct! Mummies were used in all of these ways.

use coffins. Bodies placed in coffins didn't dry like bodies in the sand, so mummification was developed.

HOW TO MAKE A MUMMY

First the body had to be washed in the ibu, or "place of purification." Next a person called the ripper would cut into the left side of the body to get the organs out. For his good work, the ripper was stoned because it was against their religious beliefs to cut a person. Even a dead one. Don't worry. It was a symbolic stoning, so they probably didn't hurt him. Much.

Then the liver, lungs, stomach, and intestines were removed, washed, and packed in natron, a substance that dried out the organs. The heart was left in place. Next, a long hook was poked through the dead person's nose, and twirled around to break up the brain so it could be pulled out. The brain was not considered important, so it was either discarded or used in medicine (more on that later). The body was then wrapped up in natron and left to dry for forty days. At first, organs were put in special mummification containers called canopic jars. Later, embalmers would wrap the organs in linen and replace them in the body after the drying period.

The body was then wrapped with many layers of linen starting with the head and neck. Fingers and toes were individually wrapped. Amulets were placed in early layers, spells were spoken, and a scroll of spells was placed between the mummy's hands. The final wrappings covered all of this.

Of course, accidents sometimes happened during the embalming process. A dead person might suddenly be without a finger or toe. Bodies had to go to the afterlife with all their parts, so what was an accident-prone priest to do? Why replace it with a wooden body part, of course!

FEELING SICK? CALL YOUR MUMMY

During the 16th and 17th centuries, corpse medicine became popular in Europe. It involved eating or drinking dead bodies. Someone might use powdered skull in their chocolate or alcohol. Human fat was used in bandages, and blood—as fresh as possible—was drunk. But the most popular ingredient in corpse medicine was mummy.

Mummies were said to be able to treat paralysis, skin eruptions, abscesses, as well as spleen and liver problems. Powdered mummy was supposed to cure epilepsy, vertigo, and palsy. It could also be applied to external wounds to stop bleeding.

The liquid from mummies soaked in wine or turpentine was used to prevent infections. Mummies were also made into molasses and eaten as a cure to the plague. Mummy balsam might cure consumption and ulcers, dissolve coagulated blood, relieve cough, and reduce pain in the spleen. It also was supposed to delay menstruation and stop people from passing gas too much.

MY TOMB IS NICER THAN YOURS

Not everybody in Egypt was buried in a fancy pyramid. The poorest people were buried in shallow sand pits, with their bodies bound in a fetal position and covered with linen cloth. But even they had afterlife swag. They were buried with pots, perhaps jewelry, and maybe a little meat. Poor people were also sometimes buried near the rich in the hope that those riches would be shared in the afterlife.

Better tombs were cut into the bedrock. An L-shaped hole was cut

The burial pit of a middle-class person, found near the Pyramid of Teti.

in the middle of the floor. Mummified animals might have been placed in this chamber, including baboons, cattle, goats, sheep, and even hippos and elephants. Though they were neither elaborate nor decorated, they indicated that those buried inside were from a higher class.

In royal cemeteries, there were mastabas, which were rectangular, flat-topped stone buildings. These covered deep shafts that led to the burial tomb. Only nobles and courtiers were buried in mastabas. Some mastabas were larger, and had several shafts, which led to different chambers that held valuables or were for use by family members. Many mastabas also had a serdab, which was a small chamber that held a statue (or statues) that looked like the deceased. The artisan Inti-shedu of the Fourth Dynasty (c. 2465 BCE) was found with four statues in his serdab.

CHAPTER FOUR

THE DOCTOR PRESCRIBES DUNG, RAW MEAT, AND DEAD MICE

The Ancient Egyptians were quite advanced as doctors, but some of their remedies might make you sick…to your stomach!

The goddess Sekhmet was the patron of medicine. Priests who were trained to be doctors in Sekhmet's temples were considered to be the best. The next level down were doctors who used both medicine and magic. The third kind of doctor had no medical training at all, and only used incantations, or chants, and amulets. Doctors also tended to specialize in one type of disease or another. The translated names of different types of doctors included "doctor of the tooth" and "shepherd of the anus."

Ancient Egyptians had colds, inflammations, and baldness. Just like us. In 2011, scientists discovered the second-oldest case of prostate cancer. This means cancer around the neck of a male's bladder. It was in a mummy known only as M1. (The oldest is a 2700-year-old Scythian king in Russia.) Some medical

This relief from the mastaba of Niankhkynum and Khnumhotep shows priests and overseers doing either a manicure, surgery, or a foot massage.

procedures are still the same. The relief on the doorway to the tomb of Akh-ma-hor shows a circumcision.

Hard labor and poor nutrition meant that the greatest need for doctors was in the villages. Egypt was once called "the motherland of diseases." Fortunately, many of their cures worked.

Some ingredients like garlic and vinegar are still used as natural medicines today. The Ancient Egyptians wrote down their medical knowledge. One papyrus from around 1500 BCE lists more than seven hundred prescriptions. Another scroll explains procedures for forty-eight different kinds of operations. A third papyrus is thought to be the first gynecology textbook in existence.

I HAVE A CURE FOR THAT

Eye diseases were very frequent in Ancient Egypt. The malachite that was found in the kohl eyeliner that both men and women used, killed germs, but more serious problems called for brains. Anything from conjunctivitis, better known as pinkeye, to problems involving the cornea, iris, and eyelid were treated with a mixture of brain and honey smeared on the eye in the evening. Half the mixture was kept to apply to the eye the next morning. The cure for blindness was a mixture that included pig eye. It was poured into the ear.

Tapeworms were cured with pomegranate root strained in water and then drunk. This paralyzed the worms and allowed them to be passed out. Other stomach problems might be cured with yeast, or by using dates as a laxative.

Patients might drink garlic to get rid of a cold or help heal other lung problems. Cloves of garlic hung around the neck were supposed to prevent colds. If that didn't work, mother's milk might.

Arthritis was eased with cumin powder mixed with flour and water. The spice called cumin mixed with grease or lard was also used as a suppository.

This jar lid has an ibex on the cover. The jar was likely used to hold some kind of ointment.

Wounds could be treated with anything from garlic, honey, and grease to fresh meat and animal dung, fortunately not all together! Burns were treated with a mixture of mother's milk, gum, and ram's hair.

Of course not all cures actually worked. The Ancient Egyptian cure for baldness called for a mixture of fat from a lion, hippo, cat, crocodile, ibex, and serpent! Just getting the ingredients alone might be deadly. Bedwetting was cured by hanging a bag of mouse bones around a person's neck. Snakebites were believed to be cured with rituals and incantations.

MAKING DIAGNOSES

Doctors poked into their patient's wounds or examined their urine or feces to tell what was going on. Incidentally, testing

A PRESCRIPTION FROM HORUS?

Some believe that the R$_x$ symbol used by pharmacists comes from the symbol for the god Horus. The eye of Horus was a symbol of protection and good health. Horus lost his left eye in a battle with his uncle Set. Thoth restored the eye (with one portion missing and filled in with magic). Horus then offered the eye to his father Osiris in order to resurrect him. The eye of Horus, also called Wadjet, was used in a system of fractions to record prescriptions, land, and grain. Each section of the eye had its own fraction. Added up, the fractions amount to 63/64. The final 1/64 might have been the magic used to restore the eye. But did R$_x$ come from the Wadjet symbol? No one is sure.

Can you see the similarities between the wadget, or eye of Horus and the R$_x$ symbol pharmacists use today?

urine and feces is still done today. But of course ancient doctors didn't have handy plastic cups. They had to handle the urine and feces with their bare hands. So gross!

In the oldest medical papyrus, there was a method of contraception that used a plug made of dung, honey, and salt. There was even an ancient pregnancy test that involved women peeing on wheat or barley seeds. If the wheat sprouted, the baby would be a girl. If barley sprouted, the baby would be a boy. If nothing happened, the woman was not pregnant.

SURGERY

Egyptians had a religious belief that the body had to enter into the afterlife whole. So surgery was a last resort. (Remember what happened to the ripper?) However, ancient surgeons were very skilled. They could debride wounds, amputate limbs, open swellings, lance boils, and cauterize wounds.

A surgeon might use trepanation, which means boring a hole in the head. Trepanation was used to treat a head wound, treat an abscess, treat mental illness, or alter a person's consciousness. Brain surgery was performed as early as 3000 BCE!

Alcohol was used in some cases to relieve pain, but opium was their strongest pain reliever. After surgery, wounds were closed with sutures, as they are today. Sometimes doctors used tape made of lint, animal grease, and honey. The lint was the base, the animal grease was a barrier to outside infections, while the honey was an antibiotic.

DENTISTRY

As early as 3000 and 2500 BCE there is evidence of dental work including drilling into teeth and extraction. Mummies have been found with gold fillings, teeth worn down to the gum, cavities, loose teeth, and teeth that were wired together.

There is evidence that fire drills were used on teeth. This tool, made of a bow and a cord, was typically used to create friction in order to make fire. Other kinds of drills were tipped with flint.

The remedies for toothaches included garlic mashed in a mixture of vinegar and water. This also eased sore throats. If that didn't work, a paste made with dead mouse was sure to stop the pain.

The Ancient Egyptians were definitely gross. They were also fascinating, very knowledgeable, and had an incredibly stable political structure that lasted longer than many others, even to this day.

This mastaba of Hesire panel shows him carrying a scribe's tools and a scepter. He was chief of dentists and physicals and chief of royal scribes to King Zoser.

GLOSSARY

amulets Small objects that are believed to provide protection to the wearer, ward off evil, and bring good luck.

balsam A compound used in medicine, often mixed with plant extracts.

cauterize Burn with something hot for the purpose of closing or treating an open wound.

coagulated Changed from fluid to thick substance, or to form a clot.

consumption A progressive wasting of the body.

contraception A means to prevent pregnancy.

debride A way to clean a wound.

dehydrated Lost water or moisture.

elixir A mixture of alcohol and water used as a base for other medicine.

embalmers People who treat a dead body in order to preserve it.

fermented Used yeast to change a liquid into alcohol.

fertility The ability to make children.

gynecology A branch of medicine that deals with women's health, particularly with the reproductive organs.

lance To cut through something.

suppository A solid mass that is inserted into the rectum or vagina that delivers medicine.

sutures Stitches used to join the edges of a wound such as after surgery.

ulcers A sore on body tissue.

vizier A high official, sometimes minister of state.

Canadian Museum of History
100 Laurier Street
Gatineau, Quebec K1A 0M8
Canada
(819) 776-7000
Website: http://www.historymuseum.ca
The Mysteries of Egypt online collection takes visitors on a jour-
ney into Ancient Egypt's life and culture. The museum also
features an IMAX film about Ancient Egypt.

Phoebe A. Hearst Museum of Anthropology
103 Kroeber Hall
University of California
Berkeley, CA 94720
Website: http://www.hearstmuseu.berkeley.edu
This museum houses more than twenty thousand artifacts and
pieces of Ancient Egyptian art, including pottery, jewelry, and
other household items.

Rosicrucian Egyptian Museum
1660 Park Avenue
San Jose, CA 95191
(408) 947-3635
Website: http://www.egyptianmuseum.org
The architecture of the museum is inspired by the Temple
of Amon at Karnak. The museum houses the largest
collection of Egyptian artifacts in western North America,
from pre-dynastic times (before the pharaohs) to the early
Islamic era.

Royal Ontario Museum
100 Queens Park
Toronto, ON M5S 2C6
Canada
(416) 586-8000
Website: http://www.rom.on.ca
In the Galleries of Africa: Egypt and Galleries of Africa:
    Nubia collections, visitors can see artifacts that show Ancient
    Egyptian fashion, architecture, writing, and technology.

The Brooklyn Museum of Art
200 Eastern Parkway
Brooklyn, NY 11238
(718) 638-5000
Website: http://www.brooklynart.org
The museum has a wide collection of art and objects from
    Ancient Egypt.

The Metropolitan Museum of Art
1000 Fifth Avenue
New York, NY 10028
(212) 535-7710
Website: http://www.metmuseum.org
This museum has an extensive collection of art and objects from
    Ancient Egypt and also includes an online site that allows
    visitors to explore artifacts.

University of Pennsylvania Museum of Archaeology and
Anthropology
3260 South Street
Philadelphia, PA 19104
(215) 898-4000
Website: http://www.pennmuseum.edu
This museum has one of the largest collections of Ancient
Egyptian and Nubian artifacts in the United States. There
are more than 42,000 items that depict both cultures.

WEBSITES

Because of the changing nature of Internet links, Rosen
Publishing has developed an online list of websites related to
the subject of this book. This site is updated regularly. Please
use this link to access the list:

http://www.rosenlinks.com/TGH/Egypt

FOR FURTHER READING

Boyer, Crispin. *National Geographic Kids Everything Ancient Egypt.* New York, NY: National Geographic, 2012.

Gifford, Clive. *Food and Cooking in Ancient Egypt.* New York, NY: Rosen Publishing, 2010.

Green, Roger Lancelyn. *Tales of Ancient Egypt.* New York, NY: Puffin Books, 2011.

Hart, George. *DK Eyewitness Books: Ancient Egypt.* New York, NY: DK Eyewitness, 2014.

Macaulay, David. *Pyramid.* New York, NY: Houghton Mifflin Harcourt, 1982.

Machajewski, Sara. *A Kid's Life in Ancient Egypt.* New York, NY: PowerKids Press, 2015.

Napoli, Donna Jo. *Treasure of Egyptian Mythology.* New York, NY: National Geographic Children's Books, 2013.

Norwich, Grace. *I Am Cleopatra.* New York, NY: Scholastic, 2014.

Pinch, Geraldine. *Egyptian Mythology: A Guide to the Gods, Goddesses, and Traditions of Ancient Egypt.* Oxford, England: Oxford University Press, 2004.

Rockwood, Leigh. *Ancient Egyptian Culture.* New York, NY: Rosen Publishing, 2014.

Rockwood, Leigh. *Ancient Egyptian Geography.* New York, NY: Rosen Publishing, 2014.

Rockwood, Leigh. *Ancient Egyptian Government.* New York, NY: Rosen Publishing, 2014.

Rockwood, Leigh. *Ancient Egyptian Technology.* New York, NY: Rosen Publishing, 2014.

Shecter, Vicky Alvear. *Cleopatra Rules!: The Amazing Life of the Original Teen Queen.* Honesdale, PA: Boyds Mills Press, 2013.

Williams, Marcia. *Ancient Egypt: Tales of Gods and Pharaohs.* New York, NY: Candlewick Press, 2013.

BIBLIOGRAPHY

Cohen, Jenny. "Did a Hippo Kill King Tut?" History in the Headlines, November 2, 2010. Retrieved June 16, 2015 (http://www.history.com/news/did-a-hippo-kill-king-tut).

Crosher, Judith. *Technology in the Time of Ancient Egypt.* Austin, TX: Raintree Steck-Vaughn, 1998.

Dolan, Maria. "The Gruesome History of Eating Corpses as Medicine." Smithsonian.com, May 6, 2012. Retrieved June 17, 2015 (http://www.smithsonianmag.com/history/the-gruesome-history-of-eating-corpses-as-medicine-82360284/).

Gifford, Clive. *Food and Cooking in Ancient Egypt.* New York, NY: Rosen Publishing, 2010.

Harris, Nathaniel. *Everyday Life in Ancient Egypt.* New York, NY: Franklin Watts, 1994.

Hart, Anne. "The Ancient Wheat and Barley Sprouts Pregnancy Test." Examiner.com, November 15, 2013. Retrieved April 17, 2015 (http://www.examiner.com/article/the-ancient-wheat-and-barley-sprouts-pregnancy-test).

Haviland, David. "15 Most Bizarre Medical Treatments Ever." CBS News. Retrieved June 15, 2015 (http://www.cbsnews.com/pictures/15-most-bizarre-medical-treatments-ever/).

Holloway, April. "From Jewel-Capped Teeth to Golden Bridges—9,000 Years of Dentistry." Ancient Origins, March 8, 2014. Retrieved June 15, 2015 (http://www.ancient-origins.net/human-origins-science/jewel-capped-teeth-golden-bridges-9000-years-dentistry-001427).

Homan, Peter. "Using a Mummy as Medicine." *The Pharmaceutical Journal*, April 8, 2015. Retrieved June 17, 2015 (http://www.pharmaceutical-journal.com/opinion/

blogs/using-a-mummy-as-a-medicine/20068297.blog).

Jones, Alfred. "The Practice of Medicine and Dentistry in Ancient Egypt." Historic Mysteries, September 9, 2011. Retrieved June 15, 2015 (http://www.historicmysteries.com/the-practice-of-medicine-and-dentistry-in-ancient-egypt/).

Jovinelly, Joann, and Jason Netelkos. *The Crafts and Culture of The Ancient Egyptians*. New York, NY: Rosen Publishing, 2002.

Kolbert, Elizabeth. "Zoos & Wildlife Conservation." *National Geographic*, October 2013. Retrieved June 15, 2015 (http://ngm.nationalgeographic.com/2013/10/zoos/kolbert-text).

Krombach, J. W., S. Kampe, C. A. Keller, and P. M. Wright "Pharaoh Menes' Death After an Anaphylactic Reaction—The End of a Myth." *Allergy* Vol. 59, No. 11, November 2004, pp. 1234–1235.

Lyons, Albert S. "Ancient Egypt." Health Guidance. Retrieved April 14, 2015 (http://www.healthguidance.org/entry/6310/1/Ancient-Egypt.html).

Martell, Hazel Mary. *The Kingfisher Book of the Ancient World From the Ice Age to the Fall of Rome*. New York, NY: Kingfisher, 1995.

Meltzer, Milton. *In the Days of the Pharaohs*. New York, NY: Franklin Watts, 2001.

Morgan, Mogg. "Trepanation/Skull Surgery in Ancient Egypt." Academia.edu. Retrieved June 18, 2015 (http://www.academia.edu/4125031/Trepanation_Skull_surgery_in_ancient_Egypt).

Pringle, Heather. "Mummy Has Oldest Case of Prostate Cancer in Ancient Egypt." American Association for the Advancement of Science, October 26, 2011. Retrieved June 16, 2015 (http://news.sciencemag.org/2011/10/mummy-has-oldest-case-prostate-cancer-ancient-egypt).

Steele, Philip. *The Egyptians and The Valley of The Kings.* New York, NY: Dillon Press, 1994.

"Tombs of Ancient Egypt." Retrieved June 17, 2015 (http://myweb.usf.edu/~liottan/tombsofancientegypt.html).

Walters, Patrick. "EGYPT PICTURES: Ancient Animal Graves From Private Zoo?" *National Geographic,* September 14, 2009. Retrieved June 15, 2015 (http://news.nationalgeographic.com/news/2009/09/photogalleries/animal-tombs-ancient-egypt-missions).

INDEX

ABOUT THE AUTHOR

Tracey Baptiste is the author of the novels *The Jumbies* and *Angel's Grace*, as well as several nonfiction books for children. She has always been fascinated by Ancient Egypt and as a child, she once tried to wrap her sleeping cat with toilet paper to look like a mummy. It didn't go well. Up until the cat incident, she had plans to become an Egyptologist. Now, Ms. Baptiste writes children's books and lives with her family in New Jersey. They own one dog and no cats.

PHOTO CREDITS